Grammaropolis PRESENTS

Vinny the Action Verb & Lucy the Linking Verb

Written by Coert Voorhees
Illustrations by Powerhouse Animation

Meet the Parts of Speech

I name a specific person, place, thing, or idea. It's a big responsibility, naming things—a responsibility that requires a certain attention to detail.

Vinny the Action Verb

Some people say I'm all over the place. Some people call me a ball of energy. I take that as a compliment, because I just like to go, go, go!

I take the place of one or more Nouns or Pronouns. I always want the Noun's job, and I hang out with the Verb and Adjective.

Lucy the Linking Verb

I'm perfectly happy to link Nouns and Pronouns with the appropriate Adjectives, but it's not like I'm going to expend a lot of energy doing so.

I modify a Noun or Pronoun. I tell what kind, which one, how many, or how much. I pride myself on being the most artistic of the parts of speech.

Connie the Conjunction

Gather 'round everybody and let's have ourselves a wonderful time. I just love bringing words and groups of words together, don't you?

I modify a Verb, Adjective, or other Adverb. I tell how, when, where, to what extent, and under what condition. I often end in –ly, but I don't have to.

Izzy the Interjection

I express emotion!! Yep, I'm always here, always ready with my commas and exclamation points, just in case.

They call me Preposition because I'm pre-positioned. I'm first. At the front. Before every other word in the phrase? Got it?

I am a chameleon. A spy. An undercover operative. I infiltrate the sentence and act as whatever part of speech suits me.

VINNY THE ACTION VERB AND LUCY THE LINKING VERB

This book is typeset in Komika Text

Graphic Design by Mckee Frazior

Distributed throughout the world by Ingram Publisher Services www.ingrambook.com

Vinny the action verb lived to express action.
I dart!
I sprint!

He loved to
jump and fly.

Lucy the linking verb did not share Vinny's taste for action.

I wish you expressed more action.
Hamlet
That is not who I am. I express a state of being.
It was hard for them to play together.

Vinny's dream was to express his action as a superhero.

Luckily for Vinny, there was a knock at the door.
It was Li'l Pete the preposition.

Vinny knew that he couldn't save Jake by himself.
I need a noun to help me move an adjective.
There are no nouns. Jake is alone.

Lucy, on the other hand, worked well with adjectives.

Jake needs us!

Okay, fine.

Li'l Pete led them all to the adjective in need.
He's just through this park, and across the street, and past the bridge.

They finally came upon poor Jake.
He's under the car.
Jake! We found you!

Lucy expressed Jake's state of being.

You seem scared.

It's Benny the adverb.

I thought I was happy, but he told me I was *not* happy.
Yeah, he becomes mean when he is hungry.
TAP
TAP
TAP

Vinny's state of being was "impatient". He wanted action, so he tried to be a transitive verb. He *lifted* the car. He *offered* his hand.
What are you doing?
Using my action with an object.

Being transitive wasn't working, so he tried using his action without any objects.
I guess you are intransitive now?
Come on, Jake! Crawl. Slither. Squeeze. Escape!

Lucy grew tired of Vinny's transitive / intransitive nonsense.
Jake, change your state of being. Be calm.
I can't.

She waved down a passerby.
Hey, Slang. Tell him to relax.
Be cool, dude.

Well, well, well.
Oh, no. Here comes Benny!
I'm gonna bounce.
Vinny was worried. He knew the adverb could pick on him, too.

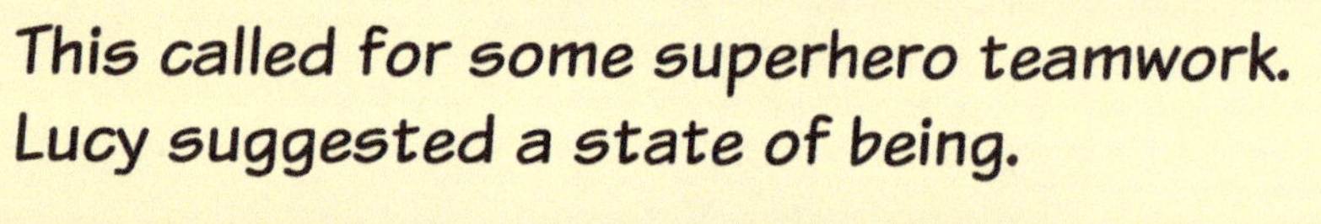

Hey, Benny. You seem hungry.

Somewhat.

Vinny gave Li'l Pete a job.
Li'l Pete, lead Benny to the store for some ice cream.
To the store! For some ice cream!

With Benny finally gone, Jake's state of being changed.
You look great.
I feel great.
And he crawled out to safety.

Just in time for some ice cream.
I don't know what got into me.
That's okay.
I want you to be very happy.

Admit it. You had fun.
Being a superhero? Yeah, it was okay.

Being in Action: Verb Notes

ACTION VERBS

They **enjoy** family time.
Mandy **ate** a pear.
Bill **walked**.

LINKING VERBS

My penguin **is** cold.
That apple **was** red.
She **looks** sad.

A linking verb expresses a state of being.

ACTION VERBS

An action verb expresses mental or physical action. Action verbs can be transitive or intransitive.

EXAMPLES

watched
danced
slept

TRANSITIVE VERBS

Transitive verbs pass action to an object.

EXAMPLES

Francine played basketball.

Shawn climbed a mountain.

In those examples, played passes its action to the direct object basketball, and climbed passes its action to the direct object mountain.

INTRANSITIVE VERBS

Intransitive verbs work alone, without objects.

EXAMPLES

Francine danced.

Shawn slept.

TRANSITIVE OR INTRANSITIVE?

Some words can be transitive or intransitive, depending on how they're used.

How do you tell?

1. Find the action verb.
2. Ask "what?" after it.
3. If the answer is in the sentence, you've found a transitive verb!!

TRANSITIVE

I ate **a hamburger.**

I ate WHAT ? A hamburger! So the verb is transitive!

I ate **before Lucy.**

I ate WHAT ? I certainly didn't eat Lucy, so the answer isn't in the sentence, The verb must be intransitive!

LINKING VERBS

A linking verb expresses a state of being. Linking verbs link the subject of the verb to information that renames or describes the subject. They often take a form of the verb "to be," but they don't have to.

EXAMPLES

My dog is a bundle of joy. My dog = a bundle of joy.

He looks happy He = happy

Both make sense! Is and looks are linking verbs!

ACTION VERB OR LINKING VERB?

Some words can be linking verbs or action verbs, depending on the way they're used. How do you know which is which? Here's one way to tell: replace the verb with a form of "to be." If the sentence still makes sense, it was a linking verb all along!

#1 This applesauce tastes wonderful.

#2 Sharon tastes the applesauce.

CPSIA information can be obtained
at www.ICGtesting.com
Printed in the USA
BVHW050946120519
547997BV00003B/7